The
Best Little Flower

Written & Illustrated by

Linda Taylor

First published by Faith Books & MORE
ISBN 978-1-939761-52-1
Printed in the United States of America
This book is printed on acid-free paper.

Faith Books & MORE
3255 Lawrenceville-Suwanee Rd.
Suite P250
Suwanee, GA 30024
publishing@faithbooksandmore.com
faithbooksandmore.com

Ordering Information:
Quantity sales. Special discounts are available on quantity purchases by corporations, associations, and others. For details, contact the publisher at the address above.

Orders by U.S. trade bookstores and wholesalers.
Please contact Ingram Book Company: Tel: (800) 937-8000;
Email: orders@ingrambook.com or visit ipage.ingrambook.com.

Dedicated to Racquel, Courtney and Ross Patrick...
the best little flowers I know.

For God so loved the world, that he gave his only begotten Son,
that whosoever believeth in him should not perish,
but have everlasting life.

— John 3:16

There once was a flower...

Who grew hidden
from sight.
No one could see him,
Not at day...not at night.

The little flower stood tall
Being the best he could be.
He stood where he thought
No one could see.

He didn't know why
   With all of his beauty,
      He was kept hidden...
         Making life seem a duty.

Often he felt lonely
   And sometimes remorse.
      But being the best you can be
         Demands living a different course.

So why did the little flower
   Stand so straight and so tall?
      Because he knew only
         How to give his all and his all.

That one lonely flower
Would in strong winds
fearfully blow.
Never breaking just
bending,
For he had a purpose
you know.

During summer storms
Which brought lightning
and rain
That sweet fragrant blossom
Accepted the pain.

Once a deer trod
　　Upon his foliage
　　　　lush and green
　　　　　　Nearly crushing his stem
　　　　　　　　So tall and so lean.

Rabbits arrived
Nibbling him with no care.

Now he felt imperfect...
Life seemed hopelessly unfair.

Bees would visit,
Buzzing in and around
his once beautiful face.
They'd steal all his pollen,
Leaving his heart heavy
with disgrace.

But the little flower remained
Being the best he could be.
He wanted to show God,
his creator,
He had enough love for
you and for me.

When the snow came...
    It covered all.
        The little flower had gone...
        No more to be tall.

Had that little trusting flower
    Lived a life in vain?
        Had the most memorable feeling
            Of that flower been pain?

When the snow melted
   As the sun shown and
      warmed from above
         It seemed quite apparent
            That the tiny reverent flower had
               died from lack of love.

The only thing left
   Where the flower had been,
     Was an ugly old knoll
        Not suited for men.

But as God's eyes wandered
Those woods with loving care

The unsightly, brown knoll
Unraveled a miracle there.

From amid that brown knoll
Sprang a tiny green stem.

It grew onward and upward
Toward God and all men.

Bursting from atop
   A delicate, lovely flower did shown.
      And God smiled as that flower
         Found he was no longer alone.

The seeds that were made
    In the preceding year
        Were scattered by wind,
           rain, rabbit, bee and deer.

That one little flower
    Who had been the best he could be,
        Now had a family of thousands...
      Because he had learned
        to trust and follow Thee.

He had died and returned
Being the best he could be.
That little flower died
For you and for me.

So when you feel sad,
Lonely, or ready to tear
Remember this flower...
And allow him to take
away your fear.

You can be the best
That you can be!
You can learn to pray
On bended knee!

Live straight
And tall.
Give your all
And your all.

Accept the storms and the pain
While spreading the seed.
Trust and follow the Lord
In your every daily deed.

Let God smile down
For you and for me.
Be the best little flower
That you can be.